The Fire Pit

The Fire Pit

COOKING AND ENJOYING LIFE ON SAPELO ISLAND

Bill Hodges and Gracie Townsend

© 2024 by Bill Hodges and Gracie Townsend

All rights reserved. This book or any portion thereof may not be reproduced or used in any manner whatsoever without the express written permission of the publisher except for the use of brief quotations in a book review.

ISBN: 9798878575461

This book is dedicated to all our friends who gather at the fire pit with us every evening.

Table of Contents

Introduction — xi
Bill's Story — xiii
Gracie's Story — xv

Chapter 1: Snacks Enjoyed around the Fire — 1

1. Grilled Sausage — 3
2. Fried Tasty Bacon — 4
3. Deviled Eggs — 6
4. Cheese Straws — 8
5. Egg Rolls — 9
6. Stuffed Mushrooms — 11
7. Crab Toast — 13

Chapter 2: Meats and Seafood — 15

1. Boston Butt Pork Stew — 16
2. Crock-Pot Ham — 18
3. The Best Steak — 19
4. Country-Fried Pork Steak — 21
5. Country Pork Ribs in the Air Fryer — 23
6. Voodoo Shrimp My Way — 24

7	Crock-Pot Pork Chops	25
8	Chicken Piccata	26
9	Pork Tenderloin on the Grill	28
10	Grilled Shrimp	30
11	Shrimp and Gravy	31
12	Quick Pan-Fried Chicken	32
13	Ike's Pork Chops	33
14	Olive Oil Fried Shrimp	34
15	Gracie's Fried Chicken	35
16	Easy and Always Delicious Roast Beef	40
17	Mississippi Mud Pork Roast	41
18	Baked "Fried" Chicken	42

Chapter 3: Side Dishes and Complements to the Meats and Seafood — 43

1	Good Old White Rice	44
2	Spanish Rice	45
3	Dirty Rice	47
4	Very Good Green Beans	49
5	Potato Salad	50
6	The Best Grits	52
7	Baked Beans	53
8	Country Squash	55
9	Mixed-Up Peas and Beans	57
10	Vidalia Onion and Cheese Sauce	58
11	Grilled Cabbage	59
12	Wilted Salad	60

13	Ho'made Au Gratin Potatoes	62
14	Yellow Cheesy Rice	64
15	Hash Brown Casserole	65
16	Grape Salad	66

Chapter 4: Sweets and Desserts — 67

1	Peanut Butter Ice Cream	68
2	Chocolate Ice Cream Pie	69
3	Grandma Jones's Red Velvet Cake	70
4	Peanut Butter Balls	72
5	Rum Cake	73
6	Strawberry Pretzel Dessert	75
7	Mama's Microwave Peanut Brittle	77
8	Sour Cream Pound Cake	79
9	Cobbler	81
10	Friendship Cake	82

Chapter 5: All the Other Stuff like Casseroles — 83

1	Shrimp Fried Rice	84
2	Enchilada Casserole	87
3	Seafood Casserole	89
4	Pork Medallions	91
5	Sauce for Pork	92
6	Redeye Gravy	93
7	Tamale Pie	94
8	Easy Pizza	96
9	Seafood Lasagna	97

10	Gracie's Sapelo "Brunswick" Stew	100
11	Squash Casserole	102
12	Crab Pie	105
13	Chicken and Rice	106
14	Gracie's Crab Stew	108
15	Burchiladas	110
16	Delish Chicken Pie	112

Conclusion and Farewell	115
Acknowledgments	117
Postscript	119

Introduction

This book came together at one of our nightly fires on Sapelo Island. Gracie Townsend and I were talking about recipes we had accumulated or created, and we thought it might be fun to create a cookbook together. We both enjoy cooking and seeing what we can create. Neither of us is a gourmet chef. We are just regular old cooks who like feeding folks. Our recipes are not difficult nor are they complex. They are meant to be easy, quick, and fun. If we miss that target, then the book is not a success.

We will try to give a little background on where most of the recipes came from. We hope that helps you understand the crazy origin of these recipes.

We have organized the book based on broad categories of foods. The recipes are mixed between mine and Gracie's. There is no particular order other than our choice on how to present these. Our lives and stories have merged around an evening fire in my yard on Sapelo. Our fire pit is situated on the marsh looking out to the Atlantic Ocean over a small creek known as the Big Hole. Every night in months with an R, we gather with old friends and new friends for conversation and a drink at the fire.

Bill's Story

I came to Sapelo Island as a part-time resident twenty-five years ago. I became a full-time resident six years ago. Gracie came to Sapelo for the University of Georgia Marine Institute seventeen years ago. We became friends around the fire, and this book came from ideas batted around at that fire.

My journey in cooking began by watching my mother cook when I was a child. I was intrigued that you could take a handful of ingredients, prepare them into a cooked dish, and have a wonderful meal. As kids, my buddy Jim Gibson and I cooked peanut brittle and other treats and sold them to friends and others. From there I joined the Boy Scouts, and my cooking took off. We started as Tenderfoots cooking hobo dinners. That progressed through Eagle Scouts where we prepared full-course meals with great desserts.

As an adult, both single and married, I cooked a great deal. Nothing was very complex, but they were typically full meals. My first wife, who passed ten years ago, was a great cook like my mom. I watched her and learned even more. In 2010 she was diagnosed with ovarian cancer and then a year later with terminal brain cancer. During the time I cared for her over three years, my cooking improved, and I added several new dishes. While it was a bad time, I could find enjoyment in cooking new things for her. In particular I spent many hours perfecting fried rice and beef brisket on the grill. In both cases I tried again and again to get it right. Also in both cases, it took about a dozen tries to get it like I wanted it. Today I do not often cook brisket, but I do cook my fried rice regularly.

When Ginger and I married in 2015, we both were fairly accomplished at cooking, and we evenly shared preparation of meals. Hers tended to be pretty complex and wonderful, and mine were typically simple from an improvised start. I believe she is the better cook, but I sure enjoy cooking for her and friends.

On Sapelo we have friends over fairly often, so the opportunity to entertain presents itself regularly. I must say cooking is fun and the bigger the group the better.

Gracie's Story

Hi, I am Gracie Mauldin Townsend, and this is my story. I moved from Decatur, Georgia, to Darien, Georgia, in 1972, about a month before I turned fourteen. Talk about culture shock! I graduated from Oglethorpe Academy in Darien, went to Brunswick College, and then spent a short time at Georgia Southern. Another culture shock!

I was way too small-town for that and opted to get married and have a family. I had three purdy baby boys and a husband for eighteen years. I still have the boys. I would probably still be married, but I just didn't like his girlfriend and some other stuff. We owned several very good businesses during that time, though, and had some really good times as well.

As much as moving to Darien was a culture shock in 1972, coming to Sapelo was just about as much of a culture shock. I came to Sapelo Island to work at the University of Georgia Marine Institute on January 3, 2007. I was the Administrative Assistant for a couple of years and then became the Program Coordinator.

Because of the comings and goings of the classes and people to the Marine Institute at all different times of the day and week, I had to live on the Island. I have loved my job now for seventeen years. Mike Lunsford has been through this whole journey with me. Grumbling and fussing sometimes, but nonetheless, he loves me and generally supports our life over on Sapelo. I might not have made it without him. He calms some of my rantings and causes some too.

My journey had many ups and downs. Losing my brother Sam, along with his friends Will and Trip, in 1981 to a boating mishap was one of those true down times. That experience made me realize that you have to hold memories, friends, and family very close to your heart. Life can turn ragged very quickly, and as my old friend Tracy Walker says, "Life can be a bugger, man." There has never been a truer statement. I get through every day making new friends. An old Brownie Scouts song comes to mind:

Make new friends but keep the old.

One is silver, and one is gold.

I met Bill and Leslie through our adventures at Tracy Walker's. He was always having oyster roasts, a fire, or cooking up something. There were some fantastic Fourth of July festivities, dang good Labor Day barbecues, and nights of, well, some things I guess we don't talk about. Good, good times. Jim Whitted and Rodie were a big part of that too. Jim was a wiry little fellow with a huge heart. He had been the captain of the *Sea Dawg* from Skidaway Marine Institute. Boy could he tell a story. As Tracy would say often, "Oh, what a time." Oops, I got sidetracked.

It was a very sad day when Bill's wife, Leslie, died. She was such a sweet lady. Bill has been very lucky twice with beautiful, sweet ladies. Ginger is giving, sweet, and one of the nicest people I know.

I now love to cook and can make just about anything I set my mind to. I also love to fish, sew, embroider, and make all crafts. When I first got married, we ate a lot of canned green beans and Kraft Mac & Cheese. I have evolved.

I have been very lucky and blessed to have met some wonderful folks along the way. I have true friends on the mainland and on the island, and I have a family I love very much!

I am glad to be doing this cookbook with Bill. Although I was thinking that this is probably the only way he will be able to get my deviled crab recipe. I am looking forward to the proceeds from sales of this book going into my retirement fund. Retirement is approaching, and I feel another culture shock right around the corner.

I hope you enjoy our cookbook as much as we have enjoyed putting it together,

sitting around the fire, and just talking about it. Much love to y'all.

Some years ago I started writing recipes in a cookbook. Many of my recipes come from that book. Enjoy the cookbook and remember it is all about friends, family, and your cherished memories.

We hope you enjoy our story told through these recipes.

CHAPTER 1

Snacks Enjoyed around the Fire

About five years ago, I began having a fire in the yard most every night during the months with an R in their name. The fire simply started as a 5:00 p.m. cocktail hour, but it has grown to be an island tradition of our small community on Sapelo Island. Sapelo is a barrier island located about five miles off the Georgia coast. Ninety-five percent of the island is publicly owned by the Georgia Department of Natural Resources, with most of the island acreage dedicated to a wildlife management area. We refer to that ten thousand acres of the island as the WMA.

The 5 percent of the island not owned by the DNR is privately owned by several families. Some of these folks represent families that trace their roots back to Thomas Spalding and his slaves. The remainder of the community and land ownership is made up of families that either work for the state of Georgia or others who have acquired land over the past fifty years. Most of the island's full-time residents live in a community known as Hog Hammock. These full-time residents number less than thirty.

The fires we have every night include members of the community as well as part-time residents on the island and visitors to the island. The fire started as a simple act to bring folks together, but it has grown to be an obsession. Every night we have a fire, and every night we have sausage at the fire. On special nights, we also have bacon as an appetizer.

Occasionally we will have other treats such as Gracie's crab bites or deviled eggs. Whatever the night brings, the treats are now a big part of the fire. As we all gather with our adult beverages, we look forward to a few great snacks.

1
Grilled Sausage

First you must start with really good sausage. I prefer smoked sausage to fresh sausage because it behaves better when cut into one-inch bites served on toothpicks around the fire.

> **Ingredients**
> Very good smoked link sausage

I cut the sausage into one-inch-long pieces and set aside to attain room temperature. Build a small fire with charcoal to one side of the grill. Once the coals are formed and bright red, put the sausage on the far side of the grill from the fire and cover the grill. It is important to not have the sausage directly over the coals because the dripping grease will burn. Cook the sausage about ten minutes, checking every few minutes. When the sausage has browned and reduced in size by about 20 percent, it is done. I remove from the fire and put a toothpick in every piece. Then pass them around the fire so everyone can enjoy the treat. *Bill*

2
Fried Tasty Bacon

Fried bacon seems pretty easy, and who needs a recipe? Well, to have bacon as an appetizer around the fire takes a little effort. So I will give you my take on one of the tastiest items you will ever have. The bacon I will introduce you to is tasty bacon, and that is even better than straight-up fried bacon.

> **Ingredients**
> Very thick-cut smoked bacon with rind on. I like my bacon for the fire cut to about 3/16-inch thick.

I use a Fry Granddaddy to cook the bacon at the fire. I fill the fryer to about ¾ full with peanut oil. Then I cut the bacon into half slices and cook about ten of these short slices at a time. I like crispy, tasty bacon, so I cook it until just a few moments before it burns. I like the rind to fluff up like pork rinds bought in bags from convenience stores. Watch the meat part of the bacon carefully so it doesn't burn. When the rind looks done, I pull it out and put it on paper towels to soak up any leftover oil. Once the bacon cools for two minutes, I pass it around the fire for the first ten folks to enjoy. The others must wait for the second batch. By the way, nothing in the world tastes much better than a few ounces of bourbon over ice cubes and a piece of this tasty bacon. That is the perfect pairing. *Bill*

3

Deviled Eggs

Deviled eggs are a great treat around a fire in the yard because they are totally unexpected. They have a great taste, and they do not sag in the humidity the way chips or crackers may. Deviled eggs are also a finger food that works great around the fire.

Ingredients
10 large eggs
¼ cup mayonnaise
⅛ cup yellow mustard
2 tbsp. sweet pickle relish
2 tbsp. dill pickle relish
Salt and pepper to taste

Begin by boiling the eggs to a hard boil. This normally takes eight to ten minutes after the water boils. I like to heavily salt the water as it tends to make the shells come off a little easier. Once the eggs are boiled, remove the shells carefully as not to disturb the egg. Once all the eggs are shelled, cut the eggs in half lengthwise.

Then carefully remove the yolk from each half egg white without ripping the egg white.

Set the egg white shells aside. Mix everything else in a bowl, including the removed yolks. Once this is well mixed and consistent, put a scoop from a spoon of the mix into each egg white half shell. These are now ready to serve. *Bill*

4

Cheese Straws

> **Ingredients**
> ½ pound extra-sharp cheese, grated
> ½ pound mild cheese, grated
> ¼ cup butter, softened just a little bit
> ¼ tsp. cayenne pepper
> ½ tsp. salt
> 1 cup plain flour

In a mixer, blend butter and cheese, which had been brought to room temperature. Add salt and pepper. Add flour. The dough will be very tight. You can now put the dough in a cookie press and make into straws or roll into a long roll. If you roll into a roll, you will need to wrap in plastic and place it in the freezer until set. This makes for easier cutting. Cut into quarter-inch rounds, place on a cookie sheet lined with parchment paper, and bake in 375-degree oven for eight to ten minutes. Cool on a wire rack.

You can wrap the straws really tight and freeze for a month or so. *Gracie*

5
Egg Rolls

The other day I was out of egg roll wrappers and decided to make my own wrappers. Well, this is not that recipe. Although one guy did say, "This does taste like an egg roll wrapper."

Ingredients
2 tbsp. cornstarch
3 tbsp. cornstarch
Chicken breast, pork, or shrimp, finely chopped
1 bag finely shredded slaw with carrots added
1 small onion, very finely diced
1 tsp. sesame oil, use sparingly
Salt and pepper
2 cups cooking oil
Egg roll wrappers

Mix 2 tablespoons of cornstarch with the soy sauce. Pour over the meat. Marinate for about forty-five minutes. Add salt and pepper to slaw mixture, set aside. Add about 3 tablespoons of oil to a pan or wok. Cook the meat until it is done. Remove meat from pan.

Add a couple more tablespoons of oil to the pan and add slaw mixture and onion. Cook until slightly done or transparent. Add meat back in and stir well. Heat the mixture together thoroughly.

Allow to cool. When fairly cool, wrap in egg roll wrappers. Place about two to three tablespoons of meat and cabbage mixture on a wrapper. Fold the two ends toward the center of the egg roll and then roll the long edge toward the outer edge to make the egg roll. Seal by placing a finger in the cornstarch mixture and spreading the mixture along the edge.

Cook in hot oil until golden brown.

These are great with fried rice with chicken. They would also be great around the fire with some soy sauce or sweet-and-sour sauce for dipping. *Gracie*

6
Stuffed Mushrooms

These mushrooms, as a good friend always said, "will make you slap your mama." But I suggest you do not do that. Have you ever heard of "I'll knock you into next week"? Well, you slap your mama, and we will see you the next year or so. Trust me, these 'shrooms are tasty.

Ingredients
a dozen or so portabella mushrooms
8 ounces cream cheese
½ cup mayonnaise
½ cup sour cream
2 crushed garlic cloves, finely diced
1 tbsp. onion powder or finely diced onion
1 cup yellow cheese
½ cup Parmesan cheese
½ cup mozzarella cheese
1½ cups chopped, boiled shrimp or crab meat or both

Heat oven to 350 degrees. Wash mushrooms and remove stems. Chop up the mushroom stems in tiny pieces. Mix together softened cream cheese, sour cream, and mayonnaise until well blended. Add garlic and onion. Mix well. Add cheeses and stir together. It should be a fairly stiff mixture. Add crab and/or shrimp. Spoon mixture into the mushroom caps and place on a baking sheet covered with foil. Place the mushrooms touching each other so they do not tip over. Sprinkle a little more Parmesan cheese over the top of each mushroom. Bake about thirty minutes until the cheese is bubbly and tan. Serve warm. *Gracie*

7

Crab Toast

This crab recipe is so darn good you really can't quit eating them. So buttery, crabby, and garlicky.

Ingredients
- 1 jar Old English cheese
- ½ cup softened butter
- ½ tsp. seasoning salt
- ½ tbsp. garlic powder or a smashed clove garlic
- 1 tbsp. mayonnaise
- 1 pound crab meat, picked for shells
- 1 package of English muffins

In a mixer, cream cheese and butter until smooth. Add seasoning and mayonnaise. Gently stir in the crab meat, mixing well. Cut muffins in half and lay out on a pan or cutting board. Spread cheese and crab mixture on each of the muffin halves or as far as it will go. Spread on a little thick. Cut each muffin into quarters. At this point, you can transfer the topped muffins to a pan and cook or put the pan in the freezer in a ziplock bag for cooking later.

To cook: Heat oven to 400 degrees. Place the fresh or frozen crab muffins on a baking sheet. Cook ten minutes or until lightly browned. Serve hot. HOLY MOLY!!! *Gracie*

CHAPTER 2

Meats and Seafood

1

Boston Butt Pork Stew

This is a recipe I halfway stole from my good friend Mike Sellers. Mike included this in his book *Goin' Dialin'*. He told us that was one of his favorite meals while working on tugboats and other push boats around the southern United States. I made a few changes and have found this to be a great meal.

Ingredients
- 2 to 4 pounds Boston butt (pork)
- 3 medium white potatoes, cut into 1-inch cubes with skin on
- 6 carrots, peeled and roughly chopped
- 1 green bell pepper, seeds removed and roughly chopped
- 2 medium onions, roughly chopped
- ½ cup chicken stock
- 2 tbsp. flour dissolved in 1 cup water
- Salt and pepper to taste
- 2 tsp. cooking oil

In a cast-iron skillet, spread the cooking oil and bring to medium hot. Brown the Boston butt on all sides. Place the butt in the Crock-Pot and add everything else. Cook on high for four hours, then lower the heat and cook two more hours. Enjoy. *Bill*

2

Crock-Pot Ham

This is a great ham. We prefer D.L. Lee hams from Alma, Georgia, and they are excellent. We have tried this with other cured hams, and they are all good. This is a good meal to cook overnight for a holiday dinner.

Ingredients
- a refrigerated ham or pork shoulder
- ½ cup water

Place the ham in the Crock-Pot. Add the water. Cook on high for three hours, then cook on low for three more hours. The ham should come apart with a fork. If it is not breaking apart, cook on low for two more hours. (Note: after removing the ham to serve, the juices remaining are great for a ham stock for cooking vegetables.) *Bill*

3

The Best Steak

This recipe is based on the T. rex method of cooking steaks used by many fine steak houses around the country. Once I got this process down, I have had no interest in ordering a steak from a restaurant. This is the most consistent and best steak I have ever had.

Ingredients
- 2-inch-thick filet mignon steak, cut from the small end of the loin
- Tony Chachere's creole seasoning
- Cavender's All Purpose Greek Seasoning
- olive oil
- salt and pepper to taste

Take the steak out of the refrigerator at least four hours before cooking. Rub the steak first with olive oil, then rub with each of the spices. Do not over salt, as the spices include salt. Place in a pan at room temperature until ready to cook. With the spices on the steak, we refer to that as letting the steak suffer.

Start a charcoal fire. Once the coals are well started, but the flame is still there, place the steak above the flames on each side for ninety seconds. Remove the steak and let rest at room temperature for about twenty minutes. While the steak is resting, bring the covered grill temperature to 400 degrees. Put the steak back on the closed grill for six minutes per side. The temperature of the meat should be 130 degrees when it comes off the grill. This is a wonderful medium-rare steak. Let the steak rest for ten minutes, then enjoy. *Bill*

4
Country-Fried Pork Steak

Over the past few years, we have cooked for fairly large groups of friends. Ginger and I like to have everything cooked the morning of the dinner so we can share time with our friends during the cocktail hour. Some dishes work well being cooked in advance, and others don't do quite as well. One we have found that works well is country-fried steak simmered in gravy. We started with beef country-fried steak, but after trying cubed pork, we were sold. This is a great southern meal that really works well when cooked in advance.

Ingredients
6 pieces cubed pork
olive oil
flour
2 large onions, roughly cut
¾ cup beef stock or beef bouillon in water
1 can cream of mushroom soup
1 tbsp. onion powder
1 tsp. garlic powder
Kitchen Bouquet or similar browning sauce
salt and pepper to taste

In an iron Dutch oven, heat about 2 tablespoons of olive oil to medium hot, not yet smoking. Salt and pepper the patted-dry pork cubed steaks, then dredge in flour. Press the flour into the pork. Place the pork pieces in the Dutch oven and fry on both sides. The pork pieces should not touch one another, so this may take two separate cookings. Once the pork is fried to a nice brown, take it out of the Dutch oven and set aside.

Add another tablespoon of olive oil to the pan and add the onions. Cook the onions on medium heat for about five minutes. Take them out and set aside. Put about 3 teaspoons of flour in the pan on medium heat. Swish around with a whisk until browned, about the color of dark peanut butter. It should be a thick roux at this point. Add the beef stock that has been heated in the microwave and stir together. Add the garlic powder and onion powder along with the mushroom soup.

Once all is mixed in the Dutch oven over medium heat, add the pork and onions back in. Stir in about a teaspoon of Kitchen Bouquet to darken the gravy. Cook for another hour in the oven at 350 degrees in the covered Dutch oven. Thirty minutes before serving, reheat in a preheated oven at 350 degrees. *Bill*

5
Country Pork Ribs in the Air Fryer

I figured this out on my own. It was raining outside, I didn't want to fire up the Green Egg, so I just cooked the ribs in the air fryer. They were excellent.

Ingredients
country ribs (bone in or boneless)
Tony Chachere's creole seasoning

Rub the ribs with the Tony Chachere's seasoning an hour before cooking. Leave the ribs out so they reach room temperature. Place the ribs on the rack in the air fryer and cook at 350 degrees for about ten minutes. Check the ribs, and if they are done, enjoy. *Bill*

6

Voodoo Shrimp My Way

A friend had a restaurant in Atlanta. One of his great appetizers was voodoo shrimp. I asked him for the recipe several times, but he never shared it with me. So I just played with the recipe until I came up with this version.

Ingredients
- 1 tbsp. ground ginger
- ½ cup hoisin sauce
- 1 tsp. garlic powder
- 1 tsp. olive oil
- ¼ tsp. cayenne pepper
- 1 pound peeled Georgia wild shrimp

Mix all ingredients except shrimp and set aside in a bowl. Sauté the shrimp in olive oil for about two to three minutes per side until they become opaque. Do not overcook. Mix in the sauce and allow to simmer for five minutes. Serve hot over chopped lettuce or cabbage. *Bill*

7

Crock-Pot Pork Chops

This recipe came about as an accident. I had thawed some pork chops and really could not decide how to cook them. So I just got out the Crock-Pot and experimented. They came out pretty good.

Ingredients
- 2 to 4 pork chops, about an inch thick
- 1 large onion, roughly chopped
- ½ cup tomato ketchup
- ½ cup chicken stock
- ¼ cup soy sauce
- 1 tbsp. minced garlic
- 5 carrots, peeled and cut into 1-inch pieces
- 1 tbsp. olive oil
- salt and pepper to taste

Put onion in the Crock-Pot. Add the pork chops. Mix everything else together and pour over the chops. Cook for four hours on high. I like this served over rice, but it is also good over grits. *Bill*

8

Chicken Piccata

I love this recipe for chicken piccata. I worked on it when my first wife was fighting brain cancer, and I wanted to cook her something a little special. We served this over white rice. It was indeed special.

Ingredients
2 chicken breasts, pounded to ¼-inch thick (If the chicken is very fat, slice to thin it before pounding.)
Wondra flour
olive oil
¾ cup white wine
1½ tbsp. capers
⅛ cup lemon juice
salt and pepper to taste

Heat a skillet to medium hot. Shake the chicken pieces in a ziplock bag with about a quarter cup of Wondra flour until the chicken is coated. Fry the pieces of chicken in 2 tablespoons of olive oil until light brown. Since the meat is thin, it will be cooked through. Set the chicken aside and deglaze the skillet with the white wine.

Cook the wine over medium-low heat, scraping any tidbits from the skillet into the wine, until the wine is reduced by half. Add the lemon juice and capers to the skillet and cook over medium-low heat. Add 1 teaspoon of Wondra flour and stir. Return the chicken to the skillet and continue cooking over low heat for four minutes. Add salt and pepper to taste. *Bill*

9

Pork Tenderloin on the Grill

This recipe is a combination of an old recipe I used many times and an improvement that my buddy Bob Thompson suggested. This pork is fabulous and can be sliced with a butter knife.

Ingredients
1 pork tenderloin
black pepper
Tony Chachere's creole seasoning
Cavender's All Purpose Greek Seasoning
3 strips bacon
butcher's twine
olive oil

Rub the tenderloin with the black pepper, Tony Chachere's, and Cavender's seasonings on all sides. Line the three strips of bacon along the sides of the tenderloin and tie them tightly in place with the butcher's twine. Let the loin sit in a pan covered with foil or Saran Wrap for four hours on the counter, not the refrigerator.

Build a good, hot fire on one side of your grill. Once the flames fall off and the coals are formed, place the tenderloin on the far side of the grill. Cook on a 375-degree grill for about fifteen to twenty minutes with the grill top closed until loin is about 120 degrees (measured with a meat thermometer).

Take the loin off and double wrap with aluminum foil. Return to the grill for five to ten more minutes until the loin is 135 degrees. Take off the grill and let it rest for at least ten minutes. *Bill*

10

Grilled Shrimp

This one is really easy. The key is to not overcook the shrimp. I have been cooking this one since my time in the Boy Scouts.

Ingredients
1 pound peeled wild Georgia shrimp
Worcestershire sauce
Tony Chachere's creole seasoning
wood skewers

Line the shrimp up on wood skewers that have been soaked in water for at least an hour. Douse the shrimp with the Worcestershire sauce. Sprinkle with the Tony Chachere's. Set out for at least an hour in a flat pan that allows them to sit in the excess sauce.

Build a fire in the grill. When the flames fall to very low, place the skewers over the flames and watch closely. Once the shrimp are opaque and slightly browned, take them off and serve over white or yellow rice. *Bill*

11

Shrimp and Gravy

This is a wonderful recipe I learned from Lula Walker and Tracy Walker, both Sapelo residents. This is one of my favorites, and it is always wonderful.

Ingredients
1 pound wild Georgia shrimp, peeled
flour
salt and pepper to taste
3 tbsp. cooking oil
¼ cup chicken stock
2 small sliced onions

In a skillet, heat the oil. Shake the dry shrimp in a bag with the flour and pepper until coated. Cook the shrimp in the oil for about three minutes per side, then set them aside. Pour off half of the remaining oil. Add a tablespoon of flour to the oil. Whisk in the pan and cook over medium heat until it browns to the color of peanut butter. Add the chicken stock and whisk together. Add the onions and sauté for ten minutes over medium heat. Add the shrimp and cook another three minutes. *Bill*

12

Quick Pan-Fried Chicken

My wife, Ginger, loves fried chicken, and I try to make this for her at least once a week or so. I try to make it taste like Chick-fil-A.

Ingredients
- 2 chicken breasts, thawed and sliced in half to reduce the thickness to less than ½ inch
- dill pickle juice
- flour
- Tony Chachere's creole seasoning
- salt and pepper to taste
- 2 tbsp. olive oil

Marinate chicken in dill pickle juice for an hour. Remove from pickle juice and pat dry. Dredge the dried chicken pieces through a mix of the flour and Tony Chachere's. Salt and pepper each piece lightly. Heat the olive oil to medium-high heat in a skillet. Once the oil is hot, place the chicken pieces in the skillet. Cook about eight minutes until the chicken is browned, then flip and cook the reverse side until that side is browned. Drain pieces on a paper towel. *Bill*

13

Ike's Pork Chops

Ike Sellers is one of the guys who lives on Sapelo. Ike is Mike Sellers's son, and this is a recipe he sent our way. We have been doing a variation of this, but we like Ike's version.

Ingredients
1 stick butter
1½ cups white rice
6 pork chops
salt and pepper to taste
2 cups milk
1 can cream of mushroom soup
1 package dry Lipton onion soup mix

Melt butter in a casserole pan. Sprinkle rice over the butter. Add chops after salting and peppering. Mix milk and soup. Pour mixture over the chops. Sprinkle the dry soup package over the chops. Cover tightly with foil and bake for one and a half hours at 350 degrees. *Bill*

14
Olive Oil Fried Shrimp

This is a great way to fry some shrimp if you don't want to take out the deep fryer. The shrimp are very lightly fried and taste great.

Ingredients
⅛ cup olive oil
1 pound peeled and deveined shrimp
2 tbsp. Wondra flour
1 tsp. garlic power
1 tsp. Tony Chachere's creole seasoning
salt and pepper to taste

Heat olive oil in a large skillet until it is hot but not smoking. Dry the shrimp with a paper towel. Shake the shrimp in a one-gallon ziplock bag with all the dry components to coat well. Pan-fry the shrimp four to six minutes until browned on both sides. Enjoy. *Bill*

15

Gracie's Fried Chicken

As I further evolved and had another baby or so, I was getting to be a good bit better cook. Cooking every day for my husband and kids, I had to. Well, I love good fried chicken, cube steak, or just about anything fried. I don't eat it quite as much these days, but dang it's so good. The basic ingredient in anything I fry is buttermilk. Total game changer in the fried world! Since I have been on Sapelo, I have learned how to make a substitute buttermilk because you can't just run to the store. Take a cup of milk and add a tablespoon of white vinegar or lemon juice. I prefer vinegar. Mix and pour over chicken.

Gracie went a little wild here. She thought her chicken was so dang good that she needed to include gravy, potatoes, and biscuits to this recipe. I don't disagree with her. This sounds pretty wonderful to me.

Fried Chicken

Ingredients
1 to 2 cut-up chickens
salt and pepper, a good sprinkle
1½ cups real buttermilk
about 2 cups self-rising flour
1 tbsp. baking powder
about 3 inches cooking oil in a large, deep pot
2 large paper bags (works best), 2 plastic grocery bags, or
   2 large ziplock bags

Salt and pepper the chicken pieces in a large bowl. Cover with buttermilk. Cover with plastic wrap and let sit for an hour or so in the refrigerator.

When ready, pour oil into the pot and turn to high heat. When hot, turn it down just a little. Put flour and baking powder into a bag. Add chicken a piece or two at a time. Holding the top of the bag shut, shake the bag to cover each piece well. Don't throw away the extra flour yet.

When the oil is ready, shake extra flour off the chicken and place the chicken in the hot oil. Cook five to six pieces at a time. Don't crowd. Let fry on medium-high heat for about twenty minutes or until nicely golden brown. You can stick the chicken to see if any blood comes out or juices are clear. Cook until clear.

Place fried chicken on a serving plate covered with a couple of layers of paper towels. Again, if you see any red juice, place back in the oil for a few more minutes.

Continue until all pieces are cooked. Turn off burner. *Gracie*

Brown Gravy

As soon as you finish frying all the chicken, strain all but about 3 or 4 tablespoons of oil into another pot or something to hold the hot oil. Set aside to cool. Put pot back on the burner. Sprinkle about a half cup flour into the pan. Put drippings from the strainer back in the pot. Stir together with the flour and oil. Turn the burner back on to medium heat and cook until nicely browned.

Make sure you get all the crumbs from the side of the pan too. If it's too dry, add another spoonful of oil to the pot. When brown, add a tea glass full of water to the flour mixture. It will bubble up and form the gravy. Stir to mix well. Turn heat down and continue stirring until thick. Add about a half cup of milk to the gravy. Continue stirring until just right. Add a touch of salt and pepper to the gravy. Serve over ho'made mashed taters.

Well, you can't have gravy without some ho'made mashed taters. I think there is a law about that somewhere. Maybe I just made that up. Who knows? But for sure, all of this goes together. *Gracie*

Ho'made Mashed Taters

Ingredients
enough water to cover the potatoes
1 tbsp. salt
5 or 6 or as many as you want Yukon potatoes, peeled and cut into eighths
1 stick butter, softened
1 cup milk
½ cup sour cream
salt and pepper

In a large pot, add water and turn on high. Pour cut potatoes into salted, boiling water and cook until tender, about twenty minutes.

When done, drain potatoes in a colander. Put in a large bowl. Add butter to the potatoes. Using a mixer, blend the potatoes and butter until smooth. Add milk and sour cream to the potatoes. Mix well. Add salt and pepper to taste. Remember, you can't take the salt back, so be careful not to add too much.

Serve immediately with brown gravy and chicken. *Gracie*

Gracie's Biscuits

Oh shoot! You can't even think about this meal without some hot, delicious biscuits. You could cheat and use Grands, but again, I'm on Sapelo and don't always have them and can't run to the store. So I make my own biscuits.

Ingredients
2½ cups flour
¾ stick cold butter, cut into cubes
1 cup buttermilk
1 tsp. baking powder

Heat oven to 400 degrees.

Put 2 cups of the flour in a bowl. Add the butter. Using a fork, combine (mash) the butter into the flour into pea-size pieces. Add buttermilk and baking powder. Stir until combined but still wet. Sprinkle some of the remaining flour into your hand. Place about a baseball-size amount of dough in the floured hand. With the other hand, sprinkle more flour onto the dough. Roll in your hand to a biscuit shape and place on pan covered with parchment paper.

Continue until all the biscuits are made. They should all be slightly damp looking. Place pan of biscuits into the hot oven. Bake about fifteen minutes or until golden brown.

Now you are ready for that fried chicken, mashed taters and gravy, and a delicious biscuit. Hope you enjoy.

All of this is great with cooked cabbage, butter beans, or little peas (not army helmet peas, though), and a big glass of sweet tea.
Gracie

16
Easy and Always Delicious Roast Beef

Back in the days when we were eating green beans and Kraft Mac & Cheese, I evolved into making this roast beef. I think it was probably on the Lipton soup package. I still make it to this day. I love the gravy with rice and a good biscuit.

Ingredients
1 package Lipton beefy onion and mushroom soup mix
2 cans cream of mushroom soup
1 can water
1 large roast beef

Mix soups together in a bowl. Place roast beef in a large, heavy pot with an ovenproof lid. Pour mixture over the roast. Do not salt, but a bit of pepper never hurts. Cook on 300 degrees for three to four hours. *Gracie*

17

Mississippi Mud Pork Roast

I had forgotten about this pork roast recipe until someone reminded me that they sure would like some. It is delicious served with mashed potatoes or red potatoes and some green beans. So here it goes.

Ingredients
2 cans cream of mushroom soup
2 packages Mississippi roast beef seasoning
1 nice-size pork roast (the kind that boneless pork chops come from)
black pepper

In a bowl, mix together the soup with the roast beef seasonings. Spray a large Crock-Pot with nonstick spray and place pork roast in it. Sprinkle pepper (you do not need salt as the soup and mixes have plenty) on the roast. Pour soup mixture over the pork. Cook on high for about four to six hours. It should fall apart. Delicious. Dig in! *Gracie*

18

Baked "Fried" Chicken

I know this sounds silly, but once you try it, you may never go back. Although there is no way in the world to beat some good ole fried chicken. This comes to a very close second.

Ingredients
- 1 stick butter melted
- 1 cup cut-up chicken
- salt and pepper
- 1 cup buttermilk
- 1½ cups self-rising flour
- 1 tsp. baking powder

Preheat oven to 350 degrees. Melt butter in a 9 x 13–inch baking dish. Place chicken pieces in a bowl, then sprinkle with salt and pepper. Add buttermilk. Meanwhile put flour in a ziplock bag. Add the chicken to the bag. Shake to coat the chicken. Place chicken in the pan with melted butter. Flip it over so both sides get buttered. Move the chicken so that all the pieces of chicken can get covered on both sides with butter. Lay all the pieces in the baking dish. Put in the oven and bake for about an hour at 350 degrees. Do not turn the chicken over. Yummy overload! *Gracie*

CHAPTER 3

Side Dishes and Complements to the Meats and Seafood

1
Good Old White Rice

White rice is a staple of our lives. We serve it with most everything. Adding the chicken bouillon really kicks the white rice up.

Ingredients
- 2 cups water
- 1 chicken bouillon cube
- 1 tsp. salt
- 1 cup white long-grain rice
- 1 tbsp. olive oil

Boil the water with the bouillon cube and salt. Once boiling, add the rice and olive oil. Boil two minutes covered, then lower the heat to very low. Cook covered for twenty minutes. Remove pot from the stove, but do not lift the top. Allow to rest for ten minutes. If you want to take this up a notch, rinse the rice with water until the water runs clear before adding to the boiling water. You can also let the rice rest for an hour or two, then bake in a covered pan or casserole dish for thirty to forty-five minutes at 350 degrees. We do both of these from time to time. *Bill*

2

Spanish Rice

Spanish rice is a revision to plain old yellow rice. We learned how to make this on the fly before a Super Bowl party a few years ago. It is a great add-on to Mexican food.

Ingredients
- 1 package yellow rice, taking about 2⅔ cups water as listed on the package
- 3 tbsp. olive oil
- 1 chicken bouillon cube
- 1 can Rotel tomatoes with chili peppers
- 1 tsp. onion powder
- 1½ tbsp. tomato ketchup

Boil the amount of water called for on the yellow rice package. Add the olive oil, chicken bouillon cube, Rotel, onion powder, and ketchup to boiling water. Boil two minutes. Add the yellow rice and flavor pack (if included) to the boiling water. Boil two minutes. Reduce the heat to very low and cook covered for twenty minutes. Remove pot from heat. Keep covered.

After ten minutes, place in a covered casserole dish and place in refrigerator until thirty minutes prior to your meal. Heat in a preheated 350-degree oven for thirty to forty-five minutes. You can dress it up further by spreading shredded sharp cheddar cheese over the Spanish rice before baking. *Bill*

3

Dirty Rice

Dirty rice is a Sapelo Island favorite at big cookouts in the yard. I am going to give you my version, but you can alter this any way you like to make it your own.

Ingredients
4 cups beef stock
1 tsp. salt
2 cups long-grain white rice
2 tbsp. olive oil
1 medium onion, finely chopped
1 green bell pepper, finely chopped
2 stalks celery, finely chopped
¼ pound ground smoked sausage
¼ pound ground beef
¼ pound small slices smoked link sausage, cooked
2 tbsp. tomato paste
½ stick butter
salt and pepper to taste

Boil the beef stock with one teaspoon of salt over medium high heat. Add the rice for two minutes. Lower the heat to low. Cover and cook the rice for twenty minutes, stirring once or twice. Once rice is cooked, set aside.

In a skillet, add olive oil and bring to medium heat. Sauté the onion, bell pepper, and celery for five minutes. Add the sausage and beef. Sauté for ten minutes on medium heat. Drain any excess grease from cooking the meat.

Place the cooked rice, meat, and vegetable mix in a baking dish that has been sprayed with nonstick spray. Add the tomato paste and butter. Stir until all is mixed. Cover the baking dish with a cover or foil and bake in the oven at 350 degrees for thirty-five minutes. *Bill*

4
Very Good Green Beans

Until I tried this method of cooking green beans, I thought fresh beans were the best. This recipe proved me wrong. Using canned Del Monte green beans gives you a very consistently cooked green bean dish. You can also use Allens green beans, but I prefer the Del Monte.

Ingredients
2 cans Del Monte green beans
1 Goya ham seasoning
2 beef bouillon cubes
¼ cup fresh spinach, finely chopped
1 tbsp. lemon juice
3 tbsp. white wine
1 tbsp. olive oil
salt and pepper to taste

Rinse the canned beans with fresh water to assure there is no metallic taste. In a medium saucepan, place all the ingredients. Lightly boil for fifteen to twenty minutes. *Bill*

5

Potato Salad

As a southerner, I have always had an appreciation for good potato salad. My mom and my wife, Ginger, make great potato salad from scratch. On a fishing trip several years ago, I had some very good potato salad. I asked the cook how she prepared it. To my shock, she said she used canned white potatoes. Up until that point in time, I had never heard of canned white potatoes. Well, I tried the potato salad with canned potatoes. It was great. Again, I think it is the perfect consistency of the canned potatoes that makes it so good.

Ingredients
- 1 tsp. olive oil
- ¼ medium onion, finely chopped
- 1 stalk celery, finely chopped
- 2 cans white potatoes, rinsed well under fresh water
- 2 tbsp. Duke's mayonnaise
- 2 tbsp. yellow mustard
- 1 tbsp. dill pickle relish or cubes
- 1 tbsp. sweet pickle relish
- salt and pepper to taste

In a skillet with 1 teaspoon of olive oil, sauté the onion and celery for five minutes on medium heat. Cut the canned potatoes into pieces about half-inch square. In a large bowl, mix everything together without beating or breaking up the potatoes. Salt and pepper to taste. Put in the refrigerator for at least four hours. *Bill*

6

The Best Grits

Grits are a simple southern dish that support all kinds of other foods, such as shrimp. This recipe varies a little from the recipe on the box. I learned this from my wife, Ginger. As always, her cooking is the best. Enjoy this great grits recipe.

Ingredients
2 tbsp. butter
4 cups chicken broth or water with 2 chicken bouillon cubes
1 tbsp. olive oil
at least 1 tbsp. salt, but salt and pepper to taste
1 cup good stone-ground grits

In a large saucepan, boil the chicken stock with the butter and olive oil plus the teaspoon of salt. Once it is boiling, stir in the grits and whisk to break up any clumps. Reduce heat and cook on low for at least fifteen minutes or until the grits are the consistency you like. I tend to like them to not flow and to stand up when a spoonful is dropped on top of the pot of grits. *Bill*

7

Baked Beans

Some of my friends on Sapelo Island love these baked beans. In fact, they all want me to make them a take-home dish anytime I cook them. I have played with this recipe a good bit. The combination shown here is what seems to be the best.

Ingredients
- 2 medium cans Bush's baked beans, any flavor
- 1 onion, finely chopped
- ¼ cup ketchup
- ¼ cup yellow mustard
- ½ cup brown sugar
- 1 tbsp. Worcestershire sauce
- 1 tsp. salt
- 1 tsp. pepper
- 5 strips bacon, cut into 1-inch pieces

Put beans in a baking dish after draining off most of the liquid. Add everything except the bacon and stir together well. Once in the pan, spread the bacon pieces over the top of the beans. Cover and bake in a 325-degree oven for forty-five minutes. Remove the cover and bake twenty more minutes. You can kick this up a notch by stirring in some ground or cut-up cooked smoked sausage before cooking. *Bill*

8
Country Squash

All my life I have appreciated good country cooking. I loved stewed squash with a bacon taste but always thought you needed to add a good deal of bacon grease. When someone finally told me that one piece of bacon would do the trick, I was skeptical. However, once I started making this and realized you got that great bacon taste with just one slice of bacon, I was hooked. This is some good stuff.

Ingredients
- 1 tbsp. olive oil
- 1 strip bacon, cut into ½-inch pieces
- 1½ pounds yellow squash, cut into ¾-inch cubes
- 1 large Vidalia onion, roughly chopped
- ¼ cup chicken broth
- 1 tsp. minced garlic
- salt and pepper to taste

In a large skillet, spread the olive oil and the pieces of bacon. Cook over medium heat for about five minutes until some of the bacon becomes crunchy. Add the squash and onion. Sauté over medium heat for fifteen minutes. Add the garlic and chicken broth. Cover skillet. Cook for twenty more minutes. The squash and onion should both be soft. Salt and pepper to taste. *Bill*

9

Mixed-Up Peas and Beans

This is simple and very good. You can also add some green beans or sweet green peas. Both additions will kick it up a notch.

Ingredients
1 cup frozen butter beans or baby lima beans
1 cup frozen black-eyed peas or field peas
½ cup frozen or canned sweet green peas
2 chicken bouillon cubes
1 tbsp. olive oil
1 tsp. lemon juice
1 tbsp. white wine
salt and pepper to taste

Place everything in a pot with enough water to cover the pea and bean mix by three-quarters of an inch. Boil for forty minutes. Taste to assure all the beans and peas are cooked. If they are a little stiff, boil covered a few more minutes. Salt and pepper to taste. *Bill*

10

Vidalia Onion and Cheese Sauce

This is a great little dish that can be served alone or as a gravy over rice, grits, toast, or a biscuit.

Ingredients
- ¼ cup water
- 2 large Vidalia onions, sliced medium thick
- 1 tbsp. olive oil
- 3 tbsp. flour
- 2 tbsp. butter
- ½ cup milk
- 1 cup sharp cheddar cheese
- 1 tsp. hot sauce
- salt and pepper to taste

In a large saucepan, bring the water to a boil. Add the onions. Cook over medium heat for fifteen minutes. Remove and drain the onions. Set aside. Dry the saucepan and add the olive oil. Heat on medium heat and whisk in the flour. Cook the flour for five minutes. Add the butter over low heat. Stir in the onions, milk, cheese, and hot sauce. Heat on low for ten minutes, stirring often. Salt and pepper to taste. *Bill*

11
Grilled Cabbage

This is a good vegetable to have with fried rice.

Ingredients
olive oil
1 tbsp. butter
1 small onion, finely chopped
½ head cabbage, shredded
3 tbsp. soy sauce
salt and pepper to taste

In a large skillet, spread about a tablespoon of olive oil and the butter. Add onions and sauté until soft, about four minutes. Add the cabbage and another teaspoon of olive oil. Cook down the cabbage, stirring often on medium heat until it loses all crunch. Finish by mixing in soy sauce and cook another two minutes on low heat. *Bill*

12
Wilted Salad

I love a good salad. I consider a good salad some nice crispy lettuce, ham or bacon, cheese, and ranch or Catalina dressing. Just me?

But it is hard to beat a wilted salad. That stuff is just so good. The first time I ever had it my friend Diane Bennett made it. Then I found out that Pizza Inn makes one similar that is also good.

Ingredients
½ pound bacon, chopped into small pieces
2 tbsp. red wine vinegar
1 tsp. sugar
salt and pepper to taste
1 large head firm iceberg lettuce, cut into bite-size pieces or chunks
½ cup good Parmesan cheese
2 to 3 green onion tops (optional)

Cook bacon in a pan over medium heat until brown, not hard. Remove bacon from pan. Add vinegar, sugar, salt, and pepper to bacon drippings. Cook until bubbling and hot. Place chopped lettuce into a large salad bowl. Pour warm mixture over the lettuce and stir well. Sprinkle with Parmesan cheese and bacon. Serve while warm.

This goes great with seafood lasagna. *Gracie*

13

Ho'made Au Gratin Potatoes

I made this for the students a while ago. The pan came back completely empty. I figured it must be mighty tasty. It actually was. I ate some also. Yummo! This is also super easy to turn into a casserole with leftover ham, added in before you bake it. Super good and a good way to use up that leftover ham.

Ingredients
8 potatoes, sliced ½-inch thick
1 stick butter
¾ cup flour
1 medium onion, diced
1 cup milk
8 ounces Velveeta cheese, cut into slices
2 cups shredded cheese
salt and pepper

Preheat oven to 350 degrees. Wash, peel, and slice potatoes. Arrange in a well-sprayed deep aluminum pan. Cover with water. Set this aside.

Make the roux. In a medium-sized pot, add butter, flour, and onion. Cook flour until it no longer has a flour taste. Do not burn. Add milk and stir well. Cook on medium heat. Add Velveeta slices and heat slowly to melt. Add other cheese. Reserve a handful of the shredded cheese to go on top of the potatoes. This should be thick and bubbly. Add salt and pepper to taste. Go easy with the salt because the cheese is salty also.

Drain potatoes. Pour cheesy roux over the potatoes and stir until the potatoes are covered with the delicious, cheesy roux.

Cover with foil and cook for one hour. Remove the foil. Add the additional cheese on top. Continue cooking until potatoes are tender and the cheese and sauce on the top is brown and delicious looking! *Gracie*

14

Yellow Cheesy Rice

I really like to make yellow cheesy rice to go with the burchiladas. So easy.

Ingredients
2 cups yellow rice
4 cups really hot water
4 tbsp. butter
1 cup shredded cheddar cheese

Preheat oven to 350 degrees.
　　Pour rice in a 9 x 13-inch pan. Pour the hot water over the rice. Add butter and cheese. Give it a stir.
　　Cover tightly with foil. Place rice in the oven and forget about it for about an hour and a half. Remove cover and fluff up the rice. It is ready to go! *Gracie*

15

Hash Brown Casserole

Hash brown casserole is another of those dishes that is satisfying and just darn good. Great as a potluck dish to take to a friend's house.

Ingredients
1 stick butter
2 bags frozen hash brown potatoes
1 can cream of mushroom soup
3 cups grated cheese
8 ounces sour cream
salt and pepper to taste
1 sleeve crushed Ritz-type cracker
1 egg, beaten

Melt butter. Mix soup with hash browns. Add butter, 2 cups of cheese, sour cream, salt, and pepper. Reserve 1 cup of cheese. Crumble crackers and sprinkle on top of the mixture. Sprinkle reserved cheese over crackers. Bake in 350-degree oven for about an hour. *Gracie*

16

Grape Salad

This is another family reunion recipe. My cousin Mamie introduced us to this. It won the recipe of the year a couple of years ago.

Ingredients
- 8 ounces softened cream cheese
- ½ cup sugar
- ½ cup sour cream
- 2 cups red grapes, cut in half
- 2 cups white grapes, cut in half
- ½ cup toasted, chopped pecans

In a mixer, mix softened cream cheese, sugar, and sour cream. Put in grapes. Stir well. Put in the refrigerator to store or can be eaten right now. Add chopped nuts right before serving. *Gracie*

CHAPTER 4

Sweets and Desserts

This is Gracie's chapter. I am not a dessert guy, and any dessert I might create is probably not worthy of repeating. However, there are two recipes dealing with ice cream that I will incorporate. Both ideas are borrowed from others and are not my own. Here you go:

1
Peanut Butter Ice Cream

My neighbor on St. Simons Island, Ann Willis, gave me this recipe. She uses it for her grandkids. Once I tried it, I started making it for my grandkids. It is easy and has been a hit every time I have served it.

Ingredients
½ gallon vanilla ice cream
½ jar peanut butter (either smooth or crunchy will work, your choice)

Allow the ice cream to soften. Once soft, put the ice cream in a bowl. Mix in the peanut butter with a spoon or spatula. Once well mixed, return to the ice-cream box. Freeze the peanut butter ice cream. Once frozen again, it is ready to serve. *Bill*

2
Chocolate Ice Cream Pie

I really don't remember who gave me this recipe, but it is easy and a chocolate lover's delight. Everything in it is easy to come by, and everything goes together perfectly.

Ingredients
1 medium tub Cool Whip
1 box ice-cream sandwiches
1 bottle Smucker's hot fudge
1 bottle Magic Shell

In a 9-inch square pan, spread one half of the Cool Whip over the bottom. Covering the pan, stack ice cream sandwiches on top of the Cool Whip. Spread and fill the cracks between the sandwiches with the hot fudge. On top of the fudge, spread the remainder of the Cool Whip. Finally, cover the top of the Cool Whip with the shaken-up Magic Shell. Place foil over the top of the pie and freeze. Once frozen thoroughly, it is ready to serve. *Bill*

3

Grandma Jones's Red Velvet Cake

One of my favorite desserts in the world was Grandma Jones's red velvet cake. Her real name was Mamie Eudoxie. No one makes them this way anymore, and it is really a shame. They were so delicious. I wonder if it's because Grandma didn't have cream cheese? Hmmm. She was born in 1900 and lived until 1995.

Ingredients
- ½ cup butter
- 1½ cups sugar
- 2 eggs
- 1 tbsp. cocoa
- 2 ounces red food coloring
- 1 tsp. salt
- 1 tsp. vanilla
- 1 cup buttermilk
- 2¼ cups plain flour
- 1½ tsp. baking soda
- 1 tbsp. vinegar
- chopped pecans (optional)

Cream together butter, sugar, and eggs. In a small bowl, make a paste of cocoa and food coloring. Add salt, vanilla, and buttermilk, alternating with the flour. Mix until smooth. Fold in, but do not beat, the soda and vinegar. Put in two greased cake pans with a bit of flour sprinkled in. Swish the flour around. Bake in 350-degree oven for about thirty minutes. Remove and cool on a clean towel or baking rack.

Icing

In a cup of milk, boil 5 tablespoons of plain flour until very thick. Add 1 cup of sweet milk. Cool. It should be very thick, like a paste. Beat 1 cup sugar, 1 teaspoon vanilla, and 1 cup butter. Add the flour mixture and beat until smooth.

Ice the cake. Add some chopped pecans, if desired. *Gracie*

4

Peanut Butter Balls

I always loved peanut butter balls in elementary school. I still love the peanut butter out of a Reese's peanut butter egg or cup. Throw the chocolate away. Weird? Maybe!

Ingredients
1 stick butter, softened
3 cups peanut butter
4 cups confectioners' sugar
chocolate, if you want it on the balls

Mix butter, peanut butter, and confectioners' sugar together. Roll into balls. Put balls in refrigerator for about an hour. At this point, I am ready to dig in. But if you want to, melt chocolate over low heat in a double boiler. Put a toothpick in each ball and dip into the warm chocolate. Let cool on waxed paper. *Gracie*

5

Rum Cake

Ingredients
- 1 vanilla pudding cake mix
- 1 small box instant vanilla pudding
- ½ cup oil
- 4 eggs
- ½ cup good rum
- ½ tsp. baking powder
- ¼ cup water
- 1 cup chopped pecans

Mix all the ingredients except the nuts until smooth. Generously grease pan. For Christmas, I like to put in individual-size pans to pass out to friends. Put chopped nuts in the bottom of the greased pan(s). Pour cake mix over the nuts. Bake in 325-degree oven for fifty to sixty minutes.

Check to make sure cake is done by inserting a knife or toothpick into the middle of the cake. If it comes out clean, it is done.

Glaze

Ingredients
1 cup sugar
½ cup rum
¼ cup water
1 stick butter

To make the glaze, you will combine the sugar, water, rum, and butter in a pot and boil for three minutes. Pour over hot cake. Let sit in the pan for thirty minutes before removing.

I flip my individual cakes over to give away. Otherwise, turn cake onto a cake plate. Do not eat and drive! *Gracie*

6

Strawberry Pretzel Dessert

I come from a large family that has huge family reunions. My cousin Joyce makes this dessert. It is against the rules to bring something with too many ingredients. This is pretty simple and very tasty.

Crust

Ingredients
2 cups crumbled pretzels
1½ sticks butter, melted
3 tbsp. sugar

Mix ingredients together and flatten into a 9 x 13-inch pan. Bake at 400 degrees for seven minutes. Remove from oven and cool. Set aside.

Filling

Ingredients
1 package strawberry Jell-O
2 cups boiling water
10 ounces thawed, cut-up frozen strawberries
1 can crushed pineapple

Cook the Jell-O according to the package directions. Add strawberries and pineapple, juice and all. Chill until almost congealed.

Topping

Ingredients
8 ounces cream cheese
¾ cup sugar
8 ounces Cool Whip

Mix sugar and cream cheese until creamy. Fold in the Cool Whip. Chill.

Pour Jell-O mixture over the crust and allow to finish congealing. When congealed, put cream cheese topping over the Jell-O layer. Place back in the refrigerator until ready to serve. This can also be put in the freezer for a frozen dessert. Just thaw a bit before serving. *Gracie*

7

Mama's Microwave Peanut Brittle

Who doesn't like some good peanut brittle? My mama makes this, and I have too. Easy and purdy darn good!

Ingredients
1 cup raw peanuts, husks removed
1 cup sugar
½ cup Karo light syrup
⅛ tsp. salt
1 tbsp. butter
1 tsp. vanilla
1 tsp. baking soda
Pam nonstick cooking spray

Spray bowl and stirring spoon well with Pam to prevent the syrup and such from sticking to them. Mix peanuts, sugar, Karo syrup, and salt in a large, microwave-safe bowl. Cook on high for four minutes. Take out. Stir quickly and put back in the microwave. Cook for four minutes on high. Take out, add 1 tablespoon of butter. Put it back in the microwave for two minutes.

Take out and add vanilla and baking soda. Stir well and pour onto a buttered cookie sheet. Have the pan ready when the mixture comes out. It will be very hot.

Be careful not to get burned. Spread on the pan and let cool. When cool, pick pan up about two to three inches and drop it on the counter to crack the peanut brittle. *Gracie*

8
Sour Cream Pound Cake

This is the best pound cake I have ever tasted or made. It is moist, delicious, and fairly easy to make.

Ingredients
- 2 sticks butter, softened
- 3 cups sugar
- 6 large eggs
- ¼ tsp. baking soda, dissolved in 1 tbsp. water
- 8 ounces sour cream
- 3 cups plain flour
- 1 tsp. baking powder
- 1 tsp. vanilla
- ¼ tsp. almond flavoring

Preheat oven to 325 degrees.

   Cream butter and sugar together. Add eggs, one at a time, to butter. Mix well. Pour in water and baking soda mixture. Alternate adding flour, sour cream, and baking powder. Mix well after each addition. Stir in flavorings.

Pour batter into greased and floured Bundt pan. Give it a tap on the countertop a couple of times to remove air bubbles.

Bake in 325-degree oven for one hour. Test to see whether done by inserting a toothpick or knife into the center of the cake. If it comes out clean, it is done. If still moist, it can be baked for fifteen minutes longer.

Turn cake onto cake plate and dig in.

Delicious warm and also makes the best pound cake toasted and buttered the next morning. *Gracie*

9
Cobbler

Whenever I have to have a go-to recipe for dessert, I always go to a cobbler. You can add any fruit you like, and it is so simple. Even I can do it, and it turns out perfect every time.

Ingredients
- 1 stick butter
- 2 cups self-rising flour
- 2 cups sugar
- 2 cups milk
- 2 cups fresh or frozen fruit

Heat oven to 350 degrees. Put butter in a Pyrex dish. Melt in the oven while it is warming up. Mix together the milk, flour, and sugar. It will be a little lumpy, kinda like pancake batter. When the butter is melted, remove from oven and pour the flour mixture into the pan. Add fruit to the batter. Do not stir. Just spread it around as you add it.

Bake at 350 degrees for about forty-five minutes or until beautifully golden brown. Delicious served warm with a dollop of ice cream on it. *Gracie*

10

Friendship Cake

I thought this was cute and should be passed around a little more.

Ingredients
1 cup of greetings
1 to 2 cups of smiles
2 large handshakes or hugs
3 to 4 cups of love
1 tbsp. of sympathy
2 cups of hospitality

Cream greetings and smiles together. Add handshakes and hugs, beaten separately.

Add love. Slowly sift sympathy and hospitality. Fold in carefully. Serve to family and friends. *Gracie*

CHAPTER 5

All the Other Stuff like Casseroles

1
Shrimp Fried Rice

During the time my first wife, Leslie, was fighting brain cancer, I worked from home and took care of her for almost two years. It was an up-and-down period. I wanted to be productive during the times she was sleeping and did not need my help. She often said she had chemo brain and wanted to just sleep in front of the TV, watching something brainless. During those times I started cooking more and working on some recipes.

For years the boys and I had been eating fried rice at a Macon, Georgia, restaurant, and it was really good. I watched them, then tried to replicate what they did on the hibachi grill. After a number of experimental attempts, I finally homed in on a very good recipe that all my friends and Leslie thought was very good. Leslie passed from the cancer in 2013. I went back to work and traveled for another five years, and in 2019 I was fortunate enough to retire. In retirement shrimp fried rice is a real go-to recipe.

Ingredients
olive oil
1 pound peeled and deveined shrimp (I prefer Georgia wild-caught shrimp.)
soy sauce
2 medium onions, chopped up medium
1 red bell pepper, chopped up medium
1 green bell pepper, chopped up medium
2 sticks celery, finely chopped
3 carrots, sliced then quartered, small chunks
3 eggs
3 cups cooked white rice
½ cup frozen green peas
salt and pepper to taste

Sprinkle olive oil in a large skillet. Heat to medium heat. Sauté the shrimp for about four minutes, then remove to a bowl. Sprinkle soy sauce over the shrimp in the bowl.

    Return shrimp to the skillet and sprinkle with more olive oil and heat to medium. Add the onion, bell peppers, celery, and carrots to the oil and sauté until soft, about eight to ten minutes. Scrape the vegetables to the side and sprinkle olive oil in the open pan area. Fry the eggs in this oil. Once fried hard, chop up the egg with a spatula and scrape over into the vegetables. Add the cooked rice to the pan and turn the heat up to medium high.

Mix everything together and cook until slightly scorched. With the spatula, turn the rice mixture over and cook until slightly scorched again. Repeat this three or four more times. Add about 4 tablespoons of soy sauce and mix well. Add frozen green peas and mix up. Lower heat to low. Cook five more minutes and remove from heat. Salt and pepper to taste. *Bill*

2

Enchilada Casserole

This is easier to make than enchiladas, which keep unrolling.

Ingredients
- 1 package corn tortillas
- 1 medium onion, finely chopped
- 1 medium bell pepper, finely chopped
- 2 stalks celery, finely chopped
- olive oil
- 1 can enchilada sauce
- 1 pound hamburger meat
- 1 can black beans, drained
- 1 can Rotel, drained
- 1 cup cheddar cheese

In a 9-inch square casserole dish, spread one layer of corn tortillas. Separately, in a skillet, sauté onion, bell pepper, and celery in olive oil until soft. Once soft, after about five minutes, add the hamburger meat. Brown over medium heat. Drain any excess grease. Add the black beans and Rotel, mix together, and spoon into casserole over corn tortillas. Pour three-quarters of the can of enchilada sauce over the meat.

Spread the remaining tortillas over the meat. Pour the remaining enchilada sauce over the top layer of tortillas. Spread cheese over the top. Bake uncovered at 350 degrees for thirty-five minutes. *Bill*

3

Seafood Casserole

This is one of my favorites. I love anything with good blue crab meat.

Ingredients
- 1 green bell pepper, finely chopped
- 1 red bell pepper, finely chopped
- 1 medium Vidalia onion, finely chopped
- 2 stalks celery, very finely chopped
- 1 tsp. olive oil
- 12 crushed Ritz crackers
- 2 tbsp. Tony Chachere's creole seasoning
- ½ pound blue crab meat
- ½ pound peeled and deveined shrimp (I like Georgia wild-caught shrimp.)
- 2 eggs, beaten well
- salt and pepper to taste
- Pam nonstick spray

In a skillet, sauté the onion, bell peppers, and celery in olive oil until soft. You do not want crunchy vegetables. Add Ritz crackers and Tony Chachere's to the vegetables. Stir and continue heating over medium-low heat for four minutes. Carefully and gently stir in the crab meat, shrimp, and egg. Mix well. Continue cooking over medium-low heat. Mix in salt and pepper. Carefully move the mix to a casserole dish that has been sprayed with Pam. Let sit for at least an hour or in the refrigerator for up to a day.

Bake the casserole for fifty minutes at 350 degrees. *Bill*

4
Pork Medallions

Ingredients
pork tenderloin steaks, 1½-inches thick
strips of bacon
toothpicks
Tony Chachere's creole seasoning

Wrap the steaks with a strip of bacon and hold in place with toothpicks soaked in water. Rub the little steaks with the Tony Chachere's seasoning. These can then be cooked either on the grill or in an air fryer at 400 degrees. Cook until they have an internal temperature of 145 degrees. *Bill*

5
Sauce for Pork

I found this sauce while on a hunting trip a few years ago. It seemed almost too simple, but it sure is good and makes any pork dish better. I like the currant jelly without seeds, but either type works.

Ingredients
- ½ cup currant grape jelly
- ½ cup horseradish sauce

Mix equal amounts of the jelly and the horseradish sauce really well. Refrigerate for an hour. Delicious on pork tenderloin. *Bill*

6

Redeye Gravy

When we had fried ham, my mom used to make redeye gravy for our breakfast grits. I always thought it was simply ham gravy and never knew it included coffee. The taste is simply amazing, and it goes well over both grits and biscuits.

Ingredients
drippings from ham steak or slice of country ham
   (whatever is left after pan-frying the ham)
3 tbsp. butter
3 tsp. flour
1½ cups strong coffee
½ tsp. black pepper

After frying the ham in a skillet, keep the drippings in the skillet over medium heat. Add the butter and melt. Slowly add the flour to brown. Once brown, add the coffee and simmer low for fifteen minutes. Salt is usually not needed. Add pepper to taste. This is a thin gravy that is great on grits, biscuits, or rice. *Bill*

7

Tamale Pie

This is my mom's favorite dinner entrée. On nights she made chili, she usually just made extra chili. Then a few days later, she made tamale pie. I have done the same with frozen chili. Janie Hodges loved this, and I do too.

Ingredients
1½ pounds ground beef
1 envelope chili mix
1 can tomato sauce
1 can pinto beans
cornmeal
flour
water
½ cup shredded cheddar cheese
salt and pepper to taste

Make chili according to directions on packet. Drain off all excess oil.

Make a corn bread–like mix with ½ cup water, 2 cups of plain cornmeal, 2 tablespoons of flour, and 1 teaspoon of salt. Make a very stiff paste. Line the baking dish with this corn bread paste. Bake this crust in the oven for fifteen minutes at 375 degrees. Remove from the oven and add chili on top of the crust. Make a top crust with the paste over the top of the filled shell.

Bake for forty-five minutes to an hour at 375 degrees. Fifteen minutes before completely done, spread sharp cheddar over the top crust and continue to bake in the oven. *Bill*

8

Easy Pizza

This is a great dish that takes just a few moments to prep and cook. When you just need a pizza, this one fills the gap.

> **Ingredients**
> 1 flour tortilla
> olive oil
> ¼ cup prepared spaghetti sauce (like Ragu or Prego)
> 20 pepperoni slices
> ¼ cup shredded cheese (cheddar, mozzarella)

Preheat the oven to 400 degrees. Place the tortilla on a cooking sheet. Brush the tortilla with olive oil, then put in oven for one minute. Remove from oven, spread spaghetti sauce on top of tortilla, and hand spread the pepperoni. Spread cheese on top and cook in oven for five to seven minutes, or until cheese is well melted. *Bill*

9
Seafood Lasagna

I love seafood lasagna and have gotten so many compliments on it over the years. I like to use fresh fish and seafood, which most of the time I have caught. It is very rich. There are two ways to make it, the long and the short. Either turns out excellent, and who is gonna know? I won't tell. You can be in the middle and make use of both. I'm talking about the Alfredo sauce.

Ingredients
⅓ cup olive oil
1 stick butter
1 pound wild Georgia shrimp (a must), peeled and deveined
1 pound small frozen scallops
1 pound fresh red fish, trout, and/or flounder
½ medium onion, finely chopped
2 to 3 cloves smashed garlic
½ pound fresh crab meat
(I put fresh whelk in it once. Freaked people out after I told them.)
½ to 1 cup flour

- 1 cup milk
- ½ cup clam juice, or boil the shrimp heads and use the stock from boiling
- 1 large garlic Parmesan Alfredo sauce (like Ragu)
- 2 cups good grated Parmesan cheese or more
- 2 cups grated mozzarella cheese or more
- salt and pepper
- splash of white wine
- 1 package oven-ready lasagna noodles

In a large skillet, heat butter and olive oil. Add chopped shrimp, fish, and scallops and cook over medium-high heat until translucent. Turn heat down a bit and add onion and garlic. Do not burn the garlic. Keep stirring lightly. Add crab. Cook until fish are flaky. Remove all from pan and set aside, leaving butter, olive oil, and juices in the pan for the roux.

Add flour and milk to the pan and make a roux. Do not brown. Add the clam or shrimp juice to the pan and stir. It should begin to get thick. Add the large jar of Alfredo sauce. Stir and mix well. You may have to add a bit more liquid. Add 1 cup of Parmesan cheese and 1 cup of mozzarella to the roux. Stir until creamy. Add fish mixture to the pan and stir well. When nice and creamy, pour about a cup into the bottom of a lasagna pan and spread out. Add a layer of lasagna noodles. Sprinkle some mozzarella and Parmesan cheese on top. Add a cup or so more of the roux, another layer of noodles, and then cheese. Keep going until all used up, ending with cheese. You may want to add some extra Parmesan and mozzarella cheese to the top.

Put in a preheated 350-degree oven and cook until the cheese on top is a beautiful brown and bubbly, usually about thirty to forty-five minutes.

Serve with some wilted salad or Caesar salad and some garlic bread.

This is another recipe that I don't actually eat, but I make a lot for my classes. It always disappears. It must be good. *Gracie*

10

Gracie's Sapelo "Brunswick" Stew

I do this recipe two ways depending on what I have cooked around the house. Leftover steak, roast beef, some pork barbecue or Boston butt, or rotisserie chicken. Just whatever happens to be in the fridge.

Ingredients
1 rib eye steak
4 chicken breasts
1 small Boston butt pork roast
½ bag frozen butter beans
½ bag frozen butter peas
1 diced onion
salt and pepper to taste
5 large potatoes, diced
1 can whole-kernel crispy corn
1 large can crushed tomatoes
1 small can tomato paste
3 tbsp. Worcestershire sauce
½ bottle good barbecue sauce (I used to use Kraft but evolved to Sweet Baby Ray's or Tommy D's.)
hot sauce to taste

Place steak, chicken, and pork in a large stockpot along with the onion, peas, and butter beans. Add about a quart of water or enough to cover the meat. Add salt and pepper to taste. Again, you can always add more later, but you can't take it out. Let cook for about an hour or so until all is tender. Take meat out to cool a bit. Add diced potatoes and corn to the pot. Let cook until potatoes are tender, about fifteen minutes. Turn temperature to medium.

Chop up the meats and add back into the pot of taters and veggies. Add tomatoes and paste to the mixture and stir. Add hot sauce, Worcestershire sauce, and barbecue sauce. You can add a bit of ketchup if you like. Turn stew to medium low and let cook for a while, probably two hours, or until you can't stand it and have to taste. You can taste along the way also.

You will need to stir fairly often all the way to the bottom to keep the veggies from sticking and burning on the bottom of the pot.

Stores well and can be frozen to save or share. *Gracie*

11

Squash Casserole

Ingredients
5 to 7 good-size zucchini and squash, cut into strips and quartered
2 eggs
1½ sticks butter
½ cup milk or sour cream
1 can cream of mushroom soup
1 sleeve Ritz crackers
3 cups shredded cheese, divided
Pam nonstick cooking spray

Preheat oven to 350 degrees. Cook the squash and onion until tender. Let cool. Mash and drain. Melt stick of butter. Pour 1½ cups of cheese and all other ingredients into bowl with drained squash and mix well.

Pour mixture into a greased pan sprayed with Pam and spread out. Add the rest of cheese to the top. Crush Ritz crackers and sprinkle on top of the cheese. Dot the rest of the butter on top of the crackers.

Bake about thirty to forty-five minutes in 350-degree oven. It should be brown and beautiful. Enjoy. *Gracie*

Cream of Mushroom Soup, Gluten-Free Option

In one of the classes that I feed at the UGA Marine Institute, I had a student who was gluten intolerant. I had to be incredibly careful with all the flour and other gluten products. So I decided to try my hand at cream of mushroom soup. I substituted almond flour for the wheat flour. It was fabulous. So I tried it with regular flour. Same result. Delicious. Another item that if you are out of on Sapelo, you cannot run to the store for.

Ingredients
- ¼ pound portobello mushrooms, others OK too
- 2 tbsp. onion
- 2 tbsp. butter
- 2 tbsp. almond flour
- 2 cups chicken broth
- ½ cup cream or whole milk
- ½ tsp. salt
- ¼ tsp. pepper
- Pinch of nutmeg

Clean and slice mushrooms. Cook about five minutes with onion and butter. Add flour and let cook a couple of minutes. Add broth and cook until hot and creamy. Add cream, salt, and pepper and stir. You can use in all recipes. Just remember about not adding extra liquid if using instead of canned soup.

Will keep for about a week in the refrigerator. *Gracie*

12

Crab Pie

I have only made this a couple of times. It is mighty tasty. Of course, just about anything with crab is gonna be good.

Ingredients
- ½ cup mayonnaise
- 2 tbsp. flour
- 2 eggs, beaten
- ½ cup shredded mild cheddar cheese
- 1 cup picked-through crab meat
- ½ Vidalia onion, diced very fine
- 6 ounces grated Swiss cheese
- unbaked pie crust

Mix first four ingredients together. Add crab, onion, and cheese. Pour into a 9-inch unbaked pie crust.

Bake in preheated 350-degree oven thirty-five to forty minutes. Serve warm. *Gracie*

13

Chicken and Rice

I asked my boys what their favorite recipe was that I made to eat when they were growing up. This was their favorite.

Ingredients
1 large package skin-on chicken thighs, or choice of chicken
salt and pepper
large slices of onion
rice, Mahatma works best
1 cup milk
½ stick butter

Place chicken thighs in a large pot with enough water to cover the pieces. Leave the skin on. Add a bit of salt and pepper and onion. Bring to a boil over medium-high heat for about an hour or until the meat falls off the bone. Remove chicken from the pot. I also remove the onion pieces. Place chicken in a baking dish to cool.

Add rice to the broth. Use your judgment about how much you need. If it looks like you have about 4 cups of broth, use 2 cups of rice. You want at least 2 to 3 cups of liquid. Use half the amount of rice than you have liquid. Give it a good stir. Bring to a boil. Turn to low and cook for about twenty minutes.

In the meantime, debone the chicken. You can discard the bones and skin. Chop the chicken into desired-size pieces or leave chunks.

Put the chicken back into the pot while the rice is still cooking. After twenty minutes, pour milk and butter into the rice and chicken. Stir. Continue cooking for another ten to fifteen minutes, stirring occasionally. You want it to be fairly juicy. Give it a taste to see if more salt or pepper is needed.

Get ready to enjoy! *Gracie*

14

Gracie's Crab Stew

My crab stew is thick like a chowder, has a rich taste, and is pretty easy to make. I love this stuff with a handful of Club crackers.

Ingredients
½ gallon sweet milk
1 can evaporated milk
2 potatoes, diced
½ stick butter
approx. ½ cup flour
1 can cream of celery soup
2 cans cream of potato soup
1 pound or more fresh, picked-out blue crab meat
1 small onion, finely diced
Tabasco to taste
salt and pepper

One most of the most important rules is to not let milk boil or stick to the bottom of the pot.

In a large pot, add milk and evaporated milk. Heat on medium-low heat. Remember, do not boil! Dice potatoes and put into a pot with water to cook potatoes until translucent. In a 12- or 14-inch pan, add butter and a few tablespoons of flour. Stir together and cook about a minute. Add cans of soup, partially mashed boiled potatoes, and stir.

Cook over medium heat until bubbly. Stir in crab meat that has been picked through for shells. Stir gently so you don't beat up the crab meat too badly. When heated through, pour in the milk. Give it a stir. Add salt, pepper, and a few dashes of Tabasco. Continue cooking on medium low. You guessed it, do not boil! If needed, you can thicken it up by putting a third of a cup of milk in a shaker or jar with a couple of tablespoons of flour. Shake well so that it does not ball up when it hits the stew. Stir quite often to prevent sticking.

Stew will smell amazing when it is ready to eat. *Gracie*

15

Burchiladas

This is another dish that rarely has leftovers. It's kinda an enchilada and kinda a burrito. So I named it burchiladas. You can use ground beef or chicken. I'm doing chicken burchiladas.

Ingredients
1 rotisserie chicken, deboned
2 packages taco seasoning
1 can black beans
1 can crispy corn
1 can Rotel
20 flour tortillas
1 large can refried beans
2 pounds Mexican shredded cheese
1 can mild enchilada sauce or make it (Very easy, I'll give the recipe at the end.)
Pam nonstick cooking spray

Here we go! Place chopped-up chicken in a large frying pan. Add taco seasoning and water according to package directions. Cook for fifteen minutes until bubbly and water is mostly evaporated.

Pour chicken into a large mixing bowl. Rinse and drain the black beans. Drain the corn. Pour beans and corn into the bowl with chicken. Add half a can of Rotel and a cup of cheese. Stir together until well mixed.

Preheat the oven to 350 degrees.

Now make an assembly line. Put out your refried beans, then the chicken, followed by the cheese and tortillas. I lay out four or five tortillas and spread refried beans on each one, then add about a third of a cup of chicken mixture and 3 to 4 tablespoons of cheese. Fold in the sides of the tortilla. Roll from the top to the bottom to form a burchilada. Place seam side down in a sprayed baking pan. Continue until all the chicken ingredients are gone.

Pour enchilada sauce over the burchiladas and cover with remaining cheese. Cover loosely with nonstick foil. Bake for about thirty minutes. Remove the foil. Continue cooking until lightly brown and bubbly.

Enchilada Sauce

Put 1 can of tomato sauce in a small saucepan. Add 2 tablespoons of chili powder and ½ teaspoon each of cumin, garlic powder, and onion powder to tomato sauce. Cook over medium heat for about ten minutes. Boom ya! Ready to pour on the burchiladas. *Gracie*

16

Delish Chicken Pie

There are ways to make this recipe quick and easy, but I assure you the extra effort is worth the time. It reminds me of going to Grandma Jones's house to eat.

Ingredients
1 chicken, boiled and deboned, or just legs and thighs
enough water to cover the chicken and end up with at least 3 cups broth
3 cups chicken broth
3 hard-boiled eggs
½ cup half-and-half
1½ cups milk
1 stick butter, melted
1½ cups self-rising flour
salt and pepper

Cook chicken until it falls off the bone. Debone the chicken. Peel and cube the eggs and set aside. Mix half-and-half with the broth and add the chicken. Put chicken mixture in a 9 x 13–inch baking dish. Add chopped eggs on top. Mix together milk, butter, and flour. Pour over the chicken but do not stir. Bake in 375-degree oven for about an hour. Crust should be golden brown. *Gracie*

Conclusion and Farewell

Thank you for joining us at the fire pit. We have taken you through an important part of our lives as cooks on Sapelo Island. We enjoy cooking, but we approach it from very different perspectives. Bill's recipes tend to be fairly short with a minimal number of components. Gracie's are more complex and bring a different texture to cooking. While we are very different, we both get to live on beautiful Sapelo Island, where our community is everything. We both get to enjoy our old and new friends and our families as we live out this great life on a barrier island.

When you live on an island, separated from the mainland by five miles of water, your approach to everything changes. You learn that your friends on the island help you get by. Independence is to be admired, but when you are out of milk, you are out of milk. We get to help one another, and we get to enjoy many of our friends and neighbors most every day at the fire pit.

We hope you enjoy a few of these recipes from time to time. We have gotten great joy out of composing this cookbook together for you. *Bill and Gracie*

Acknowledgments

We want to thank the following folks for their contribution to our cookbook. They have helped and encouraged us at the fire pit.

Mike Sellers, author of *Goin' Dialin'* and a great cook
Ike Sellers, son of Mike and a great guy
Bob Thompson, the Meat Man, a grill master
Ginger Hodges, a great cook and wonderful wife
Janie Ruth Hodges, Bill's mom
Mike Lunsford, Gracie's man
Tracy Walker, stoker of the fire
Lula Walker, one of our favorite cooks

Postscript

We are blessed to live on Sapelo Island. This barrier island is home to less than thirty descendants of the slaves of Thomas Spalding, an owner of the majority of Sapelo long before the Civil War. These folks are special people who we love, appreciate, and always welcome at our gatherings. Today there are a number of folks like us who have moved to Sapelo, either full time or part time. These folks add to the wonderful texture of our island and our home. We are grateful we get to enjoy life on Sapelo Island.

Made in the USA
Columbia, SC
21 March 2024